Presents

Little Rockers

Written & Method By:
John McCarthy

Adapted By: Jimmy Rutkowski
Supervising Editor: John McCarthy
Music Transcribing & Engraving: Jimmy Rutkowski
Production Manager: John McCarthy
Layout, Graphics & Design: Jimmy Rutkowski
Copy Editor: Cathy McCarthy

Cover Art Direction & Design:
Jimmy Rutkowski

HL00102681
ISBN: 978-1-4768-1427-8
Produced by John McCarthy

Table of Contents

Introduction...4
Clap & Tap Patterns.....................................4
Nursery Rhymes..4
Rockin' with Instruments.............................5
Fun Singing...5
Making Your Own Instruments.....................5
Your Child's First Instrument Lessons............6
Opening Act..7
Intro to Clapping & Tapping..........................7
Clapping Pattern...8
Tapping Pattern..9
Nursery Rhymes:..10
Miss White...10
Move Your Body to the Music........................11
Fun with Instruments:.................................12
Rhythm Sticks...12
Applying Rhythm Sticks Over Music...............13
Clap & Tap Pattern #1.................................14
Clap & Tap Pattern #2.................................15
Move Your Body to the Music Ants in My Pants.....16
Intro to Singing...17
La Exercise...18
Fun Singing #1..19
Learn About Timing......................................20
Whole Notes...20
Nursery Rhymes..21
Chop Chop..
Junior Jammer...22
Cupcakes and Milkshakes.............................22
Clapping a Melody.......................................23
Singing a Melody...24
Purple People Eater.....................................24
Clap & Tap Pattern #3.................................25
Clap & Tap Pattern #4.................................26
Learn About Timing......................................27
Half Notes..27
Fun with Instruments:.................................28
Shakers..28
Applying Shakers Over Music.........................29
Nursery Rhymes..30
Peas Porridge Hot..30
Sunny & Rainy Day Sounds...........................31
Fun Singing #2..32
Clapping a Melody.......................................33
Twinkle, Twinkle Little Star...........................33
Clap & Tap Pattern #5.................................34
Nursery Rhymes..35
Grandma's Glasses......................................35
Fun Singing #3..36

Learn About Timing......................................37
Quarter Notes...37
Fun with Instruments:.................................38
Tambourine...38
Clap & Tap Pattern #6.................................39
Singing a Melody...40
Parts of My Body Song..................................40
Nursery Rhymes..41
Mary, Mary Quite Contrary............................41
Fun Singing #4..42
Clap & Tap Pattern #7.................................43
Rock Star..44
Fun Facts, Learning About Instruments...........45
Piano...45
Your First Lessons with Piano........................46
Lesson 1 The Keyboard Layout.......................47
Lesson 2 Finding the C Notes and Middle C.....48
Lesson 3 C - D - E.......................................49
Lesson 4 Right Hand Notes Up From Middle C...50
Lesson 5 Playing Two Notes Together.............51
Lesson 6 The C and F Chords........................52
C Chords...52
F Chords...52
Fun Facts, Learning About Instruments Guitar...53
Your First Lessons with Guitar.......................55
Lesson 1 Holding the Guitar and Pick..............55
Lesson 2 Picking Each String.........................56
Lesson 3 Strumming.....................................57
Lesson 4 Fretting Notes................................58
Fun Facts, Learning About Instruments...........59
Drums..59
Your First Lessons with Drums.......................60
Lesson 1 Parts of the Drum Set.....................60
Lesson 2 Holding the Drum Sticks..................61
Lesson 3 4 On the Floor, Playing the Bass Drum...62
Lesson 4 The Snare, Hi-Hat Crossover............63
Lesson 5 Bass-Together................................64
Lesson 6 Bass - Together, Bass - Bass - Together...65
Lesson 7 Bass & Hi-Hat, Snare & Hi-Hat.........66
Fun Facts, Learning About Instruments Ukulele...67
Your First Lessons with Ukulele......................68
Lesson 1 Holding the Ukulele and Pick............68
Lesson 2 Picking Each String.........................69
Lesson 3 Strumming.....................................70
Lesson 4 Fretting Notes................................71
Making Instruments at Home.........................72
Piano Worksheets.......................................75
About the Author...80

Introduction

Congratulations on purchasing a program that will give your children their first experience with music. This program was designed to help children gain a sense of rhythm, timing and melody while learning about instruments and having fun. I encourage you to be involved to help guide them through the process. It's a very special moment to see your children understand music for the first time. They are learning a new language and it is exciting to see the path of success they will have. We are planting the seed of music that will grow with them their entire life. Here is how this works:

Clap & Tap Patterns

Throughout the program there will be a series of Clap Tap patterns that will help develop a child's sense of timing and rhythm. By clapping and tapping along with songs children will gain a sense of where the beat comes from in music and in the process gain coordination of their feet and hands that will help them in sports as well as everyday children's activities. Once children understand rhythm and timing they will excel at any instrument they choose to play! Have your children work on each pattern until they feel comfortable doing them on their own without the program then try to clap & tap these patterns along with them while their favorite music is playing. You'll see how much fun they will have being a part of the music!

Nursery Rhymes

The nursery rhymes included in this program are not just fun rhymes for children to enjoy they are also a way of developing a child's sense of rhythm. While the children recite them help them to clap along in time. These rhymes have a distinct rhythm pattern that will help install a keen sense of rhythm in your child's body. We also want to teach children about rhyming words and lyrics. These nursery rhymes help to show children these aspects of music that will help them understand how music is written and eventually guide them to write their own music. These are fun to enjoy together while driving in the car or just about anywhere.

Rockin' with Instruments

Here we learn how to use basic instruments rhythm sticks, shakers, bongos and the tambourine. As we develop the sense of rhythm and timing it is very important to learn how to apply it. By using simple instruments that you may have at home children will have lots of fun playing them along with songs. As children play rhythm patterns along to music they learn how to interact with other musicians, which will give them the experience to play in a band or ensemble. We'll also show you how to make instruments at home using common everyday items in this program.

Fun Singing

Learning basic pitches and matching pitches to a piano will give your child a kick-start to singing. There are a series of these exercises that are included in this programs that can help your child start to hear their own voice for the first time. This is the beginning of ear training. Training your ear will be the most important thing to help children progress in music, the more they hear tones and pitches the faster they will progress. They can even sing along with the other children to make it even more fun and exciting.

Making Your Own Instruments

Easy instructions are included for you and your children together to make four basic instruments using materials from your own home. It's easy and fun to create these instruments and start your own band with your children. These instruments can be used for the "Rockin' with Instruments" section of this program.

Your Child's First Instrument Lessons

This is the most fun and exciting section of the program! Children get their first real music lessons on piano, guitar, ukulele and drums. At a young age children need to be exposed to many instruments to see which is the most attractive to them. It is great to see a child as they gravitate to the instrument that fits perfectly with them.

Children learn the basic functions, potential and the proper way to hold each instrument. Next they get their first lessons actually playing each instrument as they get started on their musical journey. After a few months you will start to see which instruments are the perfect fit for your child. Many times, children will not just choose one but multiple instruments and singing. Encourage your child to play all instruments, they are sponges at this young age and learn quickly.

Special thanks to:
Johnny Blues, Nathan, Melody, Kaitlyn, Elyssa, Little Will and Rory

Opening Act

Intro to Clapping & Tapping

Clapping & tapping is the first step to understanding rhythm and timing. The first patterns in this book will use clapping and tapping applied to songs in time. Clap with your hands and tap your feet. Most of the music we listen to is broken down into four beat sections. For this reason we will count 1 – 2 – 3 – 4 as we clap & tap.

Clap

Tap

Parent / Teacher Notes

Clapping and tapping is the foundation to help children understand rhythm & timing. Children need to listen closely to the song and clap or tap in time along with the music. The best way to get them started with this is to guide them and clap and tap along with them. Children will vary the timing at first you need to get them to a steady pattern. Always count 1 – 2 – 3 – 4 along to help the children understand that most music is divided into 4 beat sections.

Most children will tap and clap together at first, your job is to help them separate the two motions. This will also help children to develop hand and foot coordination skills.

Clapping Pattern

We will start by just doing a clapping pattern. As you clap count 1 – 2 – 3 – 4 repetitively. Start with just clapping solo and once it is an easy comfortable motion you should clap along with some of your favorite songs.

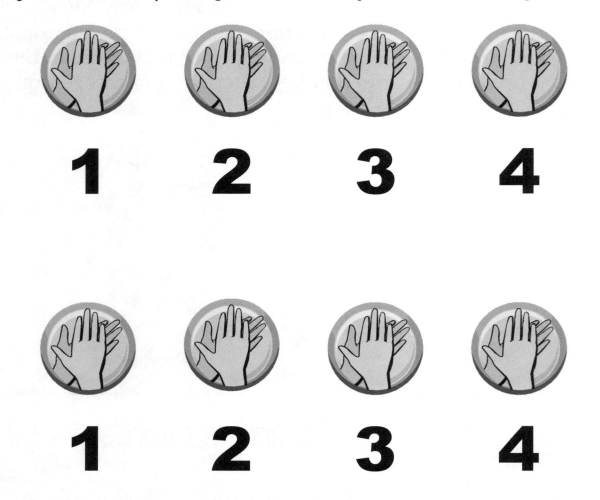

1   2   3   4

1   2   3   4

Parent / Teacher Notes

Clapping is the first skill you must have the children master. It's not just the clapping though, most children have no problem clapping it's clapping in time along with the music that has to be learned here. Count 1 – 2 – 3 – 4 while clapping always. Pick a fun song that the child likes to keep the attention span. Make sure the child is not clapping too hard because this will make them tired quickly. A soft clap is all that is needed.

Tapping Pattern

Count "one, two, three, four" and tap your foot along with each beat. Start with just tapping solo and once it is an easy comfortable motion you should tap along with some of your favorite songs.

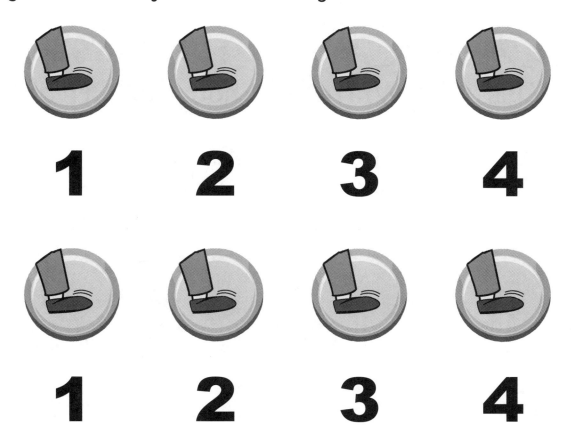

1   **2**   **3**   **4**

1   **2**   **3**   **4**

Parent / Teacher Notes

Tapping can be done two ways, one by just picking up the entire foot and tapping down at the ball of the foot. The second is holding the heal down and moving the front of the foot up and down. Make sure the knee is bent some children try to keep the leg extended out which is not the best form.

Tapping like clapping has to be done while counting 1 – 2 – 3 – 4 and in time with music. Guide the child by tapping along with them.

Nursery Rhymes: Miss White

Clap along and recite the rhyme. Notice the rhyming words.

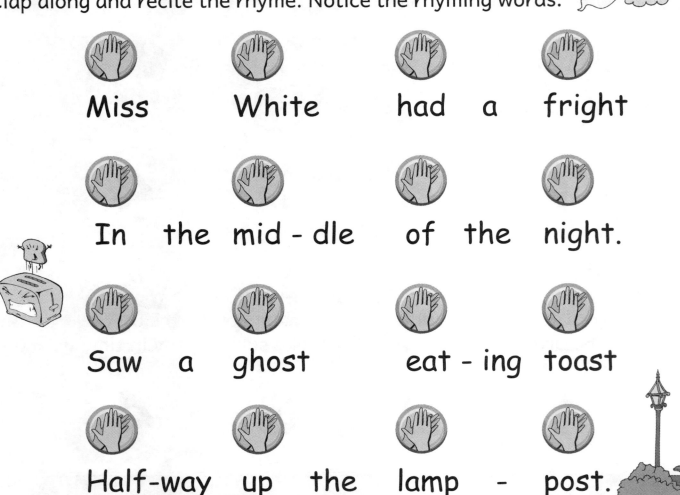

Miss White had a fright

In the mid - dle of the night.

Saw a ghost eat - ing toast

Half-way up the lamp - post.

Parent / Teacher Notes

The nursery rhyme Miss White has several important elements that will help your children musically. Clap along with the count of 1 – 2 – 3 – 4 as you recite the rhyme, this will help them to understand lyrical rhythm or singing in time with the beat. Notice how there are 4 claps per line. The second thing to talk to the children about this is the rhyming words. Explain how "white, fright and night" and "ghost, toast and post" rhyme. Have the children think of other rhyming words.

Move Your Body to the Music

Your body is the rhythm keeper! Move your body along with the music and feel the rhythm. As the song is playing go through these motions to have some fun and get your body clock ticking.

Move Your Head To The Music: Start nodding yes in time and then no. Bobbing your head is common and easy way to feel the music.

Swim To The Music: Move your arms in a swimming motion along with the music. You can move around the room as you are swimming. Make sure to do this in time and count 1 – 2 – 3 – 4.

Flap Your Arms Like A Bird: In time move your arms in a flapping motion. You can be a big bird a small bird or even a penguin.

Raise The Roof: Jump up and down and push your arms up towards the ceiling like you are pushing the roof up. Make sure to stay in time with the music.

Kick You Feet Out: One foot at a time kick your feet out in front of you.

Move Your Entire Body: Can you move your entire body to the music? Yes you can! Move you hands, feet, head and arms all while keeping in time with the music.

Parent / Teacher Notes

This is a fun exercise for children. Pick a favorite song the children like or choose one from our suggested list. Prepare an open area with no obstacles that children can trip on. Start with the list of movements and do each in time with the music while counting 1 – 2 – 3 – 4. Switch movements every 20 seconds or so.

Fun with Instruments: Rhythm Sticks

Rhythm sticks are a simple musical instrument that can be used to play rhythmic patterns. Striking them together generates the sound.

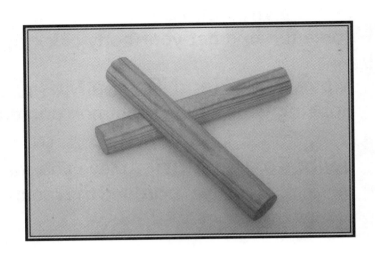

Hold the striker stick with your dominant hand and the stick that will be hit with the other like shown in the picture. Hold the sticks loosely to get a louder sound.

Parent / Teacher Notes

Rhythm sticks are one of the easiest percussion instruments to have children use. Make sure the striking stick is in the dominate hand. Have children hold both sticks loosely because they will be louder.

Applying Rhythm Sticks Over Music

Now let's play the rhythm sticks along with a song. Count 1 – 2 – 3 – 4 while hitting the sticks together along with the song. When you are ready and have mastered the single beat timing try double time striking, this is when you strike them twice for each beat.

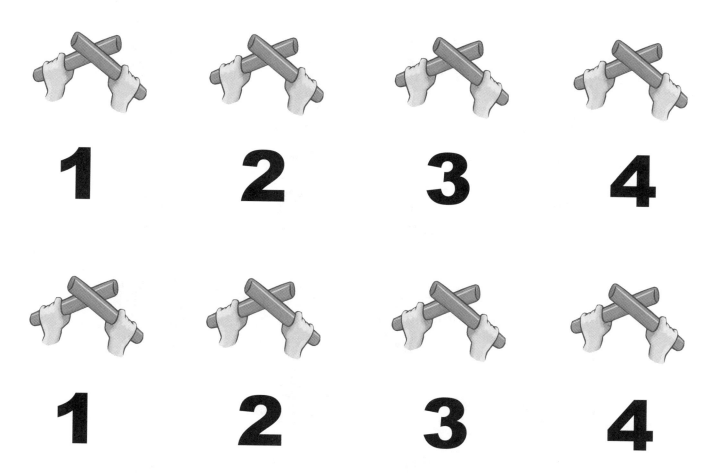

Parent / Teacher Notes

As with all percussion instruments count 1 – 2 – 3 – 4 while playing them along with a song of the childrens choice. Have the children play "Double-time" when the chorus of the song comes up, this is playing them 2 times for each count.

Clap & Tap Pattern #1

Now lets combine clapping and tapping to make a musical pattern. Tap and clap back and forth in a steady rhythm. Apply this pattern over any song. Make sure to count 1 – 2 – 3 – 4 and have the children count along with you.

Parent / Teacher Notes

This is the first pattern that combines tapping & clapping. This is an important lesson to make sure the student can coordinate foot and hand movement back and forth. It will not be easy for many children so be patient and start very slowly. Once they get the coordination have the children count 1 – 2 – 3 – 4 along with the pattern.

Clap & Tap Pattern #2

For this pattern you will tap twice and then clap. There is a rest on beat 4. Once the children can perform this pattern repetitively apply this along with the song We Will Rock You.

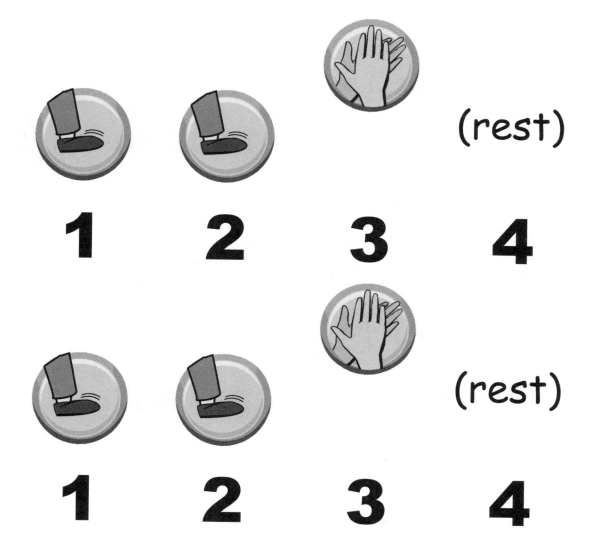

(rest)

1   **2**   **3**   **4**

(rest)

1   **2**   **3**   **4**

Parent / Teacher Notes

The thing you have to help the children with is waiting an extra beat after the clap. Applying the pattern along with "We Will Rock You" will really help the children get the pattern quickly. Also have them sing along with the song.

Move Your Body to the Music
Ants in My Pants

Here is a fun song to get your body clock rocking! Move as if you had ants in your pants and shake your body to the music! Remember that the more you feel the music the better you can play it.

I got ants in my pants,

Feel them all around.

I got ants in my pants

Jump up and jump down.

I got ants in my pants,

I gotta get them out.

I got ants in my pants.

Everybody shout!

Parent / Teacher Notes

Use the corresponding audio track to play the song for the children. Have the children sing along and move their body to the music as if they really had ants in their pants. Make this a fun interactive lesson!

Intro to Singing

In order to sing you need to breathe in deep and control your airflow. Take a deep breath in and fill your tummy up before you start to sing. As you sing make sure to let the air out slowly as you sing the notes.

Parent / Teacher Notes

Breath control is important for children to understand to start singing. Have the children take a big breath and let the air out as slow as they can. This way of breathing is what they need to understand to get started.

La Exercise

Let's sing a fun breath control exercise. Take a deep breath in and sing "La" and hold the note as long as you can. Hold your hand in front of your mouth and feel the air coming out. Make sure it is coming out slowly; this will allow you to hold the note longer.

Parent / Teacher Notes

Now that they have practice breathing in deeply and letting the air out slowly the next step is to put pitch in the mix. Using a "La" sound have the children take a deep breath in and hold the sound as long as they can. I like to make it a contest and see who can hold the note out longest.

Fun Singing #1

A melody is made up of a series of musical notes. Sing the following melody using the breath control you learned in the previous lesson. Use the audio track to sing along with the exercise.

Do Re Mi   (Do) (Re) (Mi)

Mi Re Do   (Mi) (Re) (Do)

Do Mi Re   (Do) (Mi) (Re)

Re Mi Do   (Re) (Mi) (Do)

Parent / Teacher Notes

If you don't have a piano or guitar use the backing track to have the children sing along with this lesson. Also, use your hand to dictate the pitch going up and down. Have the children do the same hand movements. This is important because it will help children learn about pitch, high and low notes.

Learn About Timing
Whole Notes

A whole note receives 4 beats of sound. See the whole note below looks like a hollow circle or a doughnut. If you were singing or playing a whole note you would hold the notes pitch for 4 beats.

Let's play and sing whole notes now.

1   2   3   4

Parent / Teacher Notes

Children will now start to learn about note types. They need to memorize what the note looks like, a hollow circle or doughnut. They also need to know that it gets 4 beats. Have the children sing a "La" sound and hold it for 4 beats.

Nursery Rhymes
Chop Chop

What can you think of to put in our soup? Pick your favorite meats or veggies. Make sure to chop each ingredient up, pour each into the pot and then drink up the soup at the end!

Chop, chop, choppity chop.

Cut off the bottom, cut off the top.

What we have left we put in the pot.

Chop, chop, choppity chop.

Parent / Teacher Notes

This rhythm has a routine as well. Watch the corresponding video lesson to see the routine and either do it yourself or use the video with the children.

Junior Jammer

Cupcakes and Milkshakes

Here is another fun song the Little Rockers class made up together. Try to make up your own songs as well. Use rhyming words and create a fun melody.

Cupcakes and milkshakes,
I love them every day.
Cupcakes and milkshakes,
Let's eat them, hurray!
Cupcakes and milkshakes,
They taste so good.
Cupcakes and milkshakes,
The way we know they should.

Parent / Teacher Notes

Make sure to use the audio track along with this song. Have the children sing along while moving their body to the music. I always try to have the children make up their own version or song as well. This helps to teach them to be creative.

Clapping a Melody

Clapping along with melodies will help you to understand rhythm and timing. Have fun with Happy Birthday and clap the melody. Pick someone in the class to have a pretend birthday and have them blow the candles out too.

Hap - py   Birth - day   to   you.

Hap - py   Birth - day   to   you.

Hap - py   Birth - day   dear   John - ny.

Hap - py   Birth - day   to   you.

Parent / Teacher Notes

Guide the children to clap along with the song. They will be clapping on each syllable. Also have the children sing the song. To make it fun pretend it's the birthday of someone in the room. Have them blow out the imaginary candles at the end!

Singing a Melody
Purple People Eater

Here is a fun melody to sing together. Clap along as you sing.

It was a one-eyed, one-horned,
flyin' purple people eater.
(One-eyed, one-horned,
flyin' purple people eater).
A one-eyed, one-horned,
flyin' purple people eater.
Sure looks strange to me.

Parent / Teacher Notes

Children will sing and clap along with this fun song. Have the children move their body to the music as well. You can even have them walk around as they sing.

Clap & Tap Pattern #3

In pattern #3 you will tap and then clap three times. As in all clap tap patterns count 1 – 2 – 3 – 4 as you perform the pattern.

Clap & Tap Pattern #4

For this next pattern, tap twice in a row and then clap twice in a row. You should clap and tap this pattern along with some of your favorite songs.

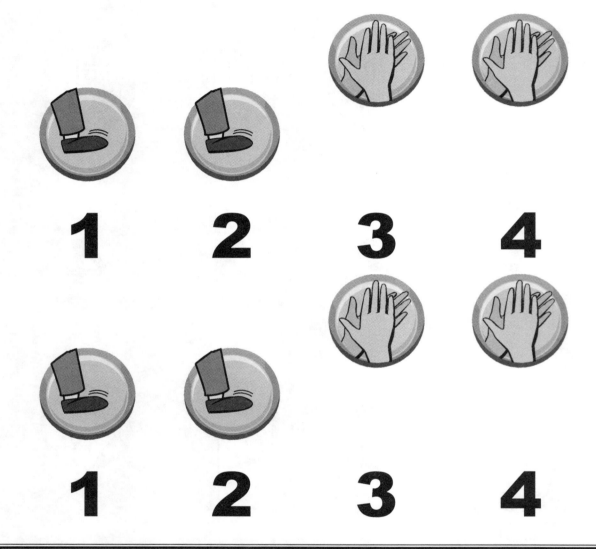

Parent / Teacher Notes

With clap & tap patterns it is very important to keep a steady rhythm. Children will tend to speed up on the three claps. Do the pattern along with the children until they are comfortable then have them do the pattern on their own. Next they should apply the pattern along with a song of your choice.

Learn About Timing
Half Notes

A half note receives 2 beats of sound. Take a look at the half note below, it has a hollow head like the whole note but also has a stem. If you were playing or singing a half note you would hold the notes pitch for 2 counts.

Try singing or playing half notes in a row to get used to this timing.

1   2   3   4

Parent / Teacher Notes

The children should know that the half note has a hollow head and a stem. Using a "La" sing half notes along with the children. Have them tap their foot to count the two beats for each note.

Fun with Instruments: Shakers

Shakers are percussion instruments. By shaking them in time with the music you can create rhythms.

Hold one shaker in each hand and push your hands straight out in front of you repetitively to create the percussive sound. Shakers come in many shapes and sizes. Maracas are shakers too.

Parent / Teacher Notes

Each child should have two shakers, one in each hand. The basic form is to have them push forward with both hands at the same time.

Applying Shakers Over Music

Now let's play the shakers along with a song. Count 1 – 2 – 3 – 4 while shaking the shakers with the song. When you are ready and have mastered the basic motion try some of the other movements listed here:

Shake up in the air.

Shake towards the floor.

One arm up, one arm down.

Shake them in crazy wild movements.

Parent / Teacher Notes

Play a familiar song and have the children shake the patterns listed above in time to the music. I also like to have the children stand up and move their body as they shake them.

Nursery Rhymes
Peas Porridge Hot

Rhymes are great ways to practice rhythm and timing. Clap and tap as you recite this rhythm.

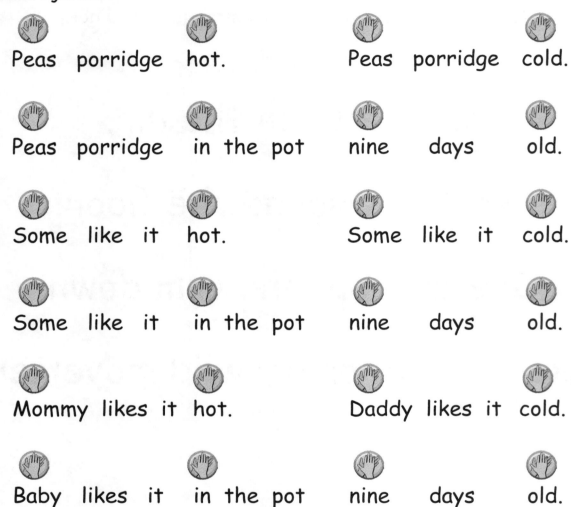

Peas porridge hot.   Peas porridge cold.

Peas porridge in the pot   nine days old.

Some like it hot.   Some like it cold.

Some like it in the pot   nine days old.

Mommy likes it hot.   Daddy likes it cold.

Baby likes it in the pot   nine days old.

Parent / Teacher Notes

For this nursery rhythm, the children will be clapping on the counts of 1 – 2 – 3 – 4. Demonstrate the clapping for the children and then have them follow along. I do this repetitively with the children for a few minutes.

Sunny & Rainy Day Sounds

Songs are written using different types of chords. The two main types of chords are called Major and Minor chords.

Major chords are happy sounding and I call them the Sunny day chords. Minor chords are sad and I call these the Rainy Day chords. People use different types of chords to write songs and create happy and sad emotions.

Major Chords

Happy Sounding

Minor Chords

Sad Sounding

Parent / Teacher Notes

If you are able to play an instrument, play a series of major and minor chords for the children and have them try to tell you if it is major or minor. If you can't play an instrument use the accompanying audio track.

Fun Singing #2

Here is another singing melody exercise. If you practice this every day, it will help you to sing better. Match the pitches with the audio track.

La   la   la   la   la

(La) (la) (la) (la) (la)

Parent / Teacher Notes

Use the accompanying audio track to have the children sing this exercise. Have them repeat the pattern and pay attention to make sure they are matching the correct pitch. If you can play piano or guitar play a C Major arpeggio. Then move up the triads of the C major scale.

Clapping a Melody
Twinkle, Twinkle Little Star

This is a classic rhyme melody. Clap and sing along with the song.

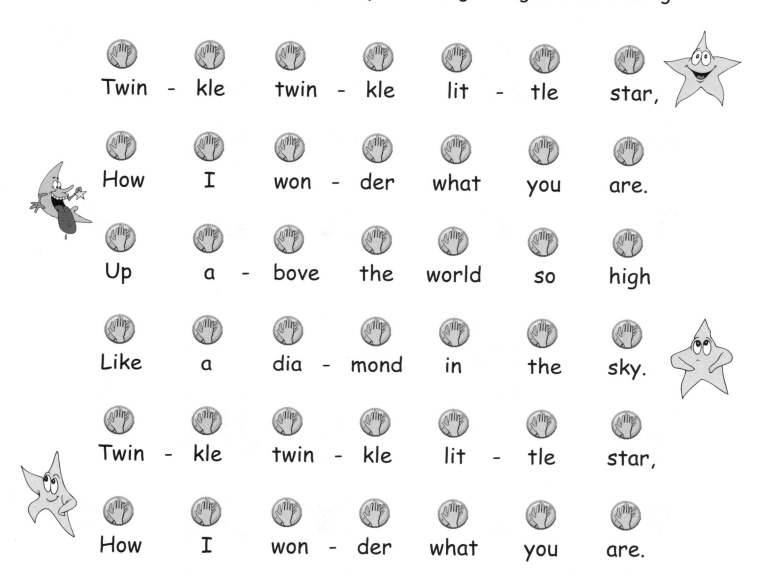

Twin - kle   twin - kle   lit - tle   star,

How   I   won - der   what   you   are.

Up   a - bove   the   world   so   high

Like   a   dia - mond   in   the   sky.

Twin - kle   twin - kle   lit - tle   star,

How   I   won - der   what   you   are.

Parent / Teacher Notes

In this rhyme children will clap on each syllable. Most children will know this rhyme already so concentrate on clapping in time.

Clap & Tap Pattern #5

This pattern is used in many songs. The tapping represents the Bass Drum, and the clapping represents the Snare drum. The count is slightly different adding one more count as follows: 1 – 2 – 3 and 4.

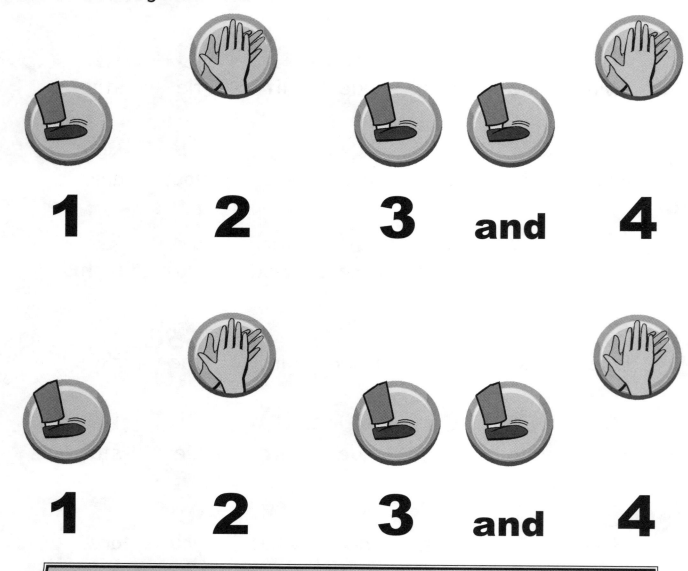

1   2   3   and   4

1   2   3   and   4

Parent / Teacher Notes

This clap & tap pattern is one that follows a common drum beat used in many hit songs. The tapping is the bass drum and the clapping is the snare drum in the pattern. Once you have the children doing the pattern have them apply it over a popular song.

Nursery Rhymes
Grandma's Glasses

Here is another great rhyme to have fun with. Use the audio track to hear the timing and melody.

These are Grandma's glasses,

This is Grandma's hat.

This is how she folds her hands

And holds them in her lap.

These are Grandpa's glasses,

This is Grandpa's hat.

This is how he folds his arms.

Oh, what do you think of that?

Parent / Teacher Notes

This rhyme has a fun follow along routine. Watch the video for this lesson to get the routine to use with the students.

Fun Singing #3

Dynamics are how loud or soft notes are played or sung. In this lesson you will sing "Softly" and then "Loudly." You also will sing a note and hold the pitch as long as you can as you did in a past lesson.

Holding Notes

Take a deep breath and sing a note holding the pitch for as long as you can. Remember to not let your air out quickly.

Singing Softly

Next sing the same note softly. This is called dynamics.

Singing Loudly

Now breathe in as much air as you can and sing the same note LOUDLY.

Parent / Teacher Notes

These singing exercises help children understand dynamics and breath control. Children usually let out a lot of air when singing. It is VERY important for them to learn how to let air out slowly while singing to gain tone and power in the voice. Have the children hold their hand in front of their mouth to feel how much air comes out.

Learn About Timing
Quarter Notes

A quarter note receives 1 beat of sound. See the quarter note to the right, it has a solid head and a stem.

If you were singing or playing a quarter note you would hold the note's pitch for 1 beat. Let's play and sing quarter notes now.

Parent / Teacher Notes

Quarter notes are sang or played on the count of 1 – 2 – 3 – 4. Have the children sing "La" in quarter note timing. They can also use any percussion instrument to play the quarter notes.

Fun with Instruments: Tambourine

Another fun percussion instrument is a tambourine. Some tambourines have a striking surface like a drum, other just have the bells in a handle shaped casing. Hold the tambourine in your dominate hand and strike it gently against the other hand to make a percussive sound. Do this repetitively to make a rhythm pattern.

1   **2**   **3**   **4**

Parent / Teacher Notes

Children should hold the tambourine with their dominant hand and strike it against the other hand. Make sure to enforce to not hit too hard. Play the tambourine along with any song the children like in all the timing variations, quarter, half and whole notes.

Clap & Tap Pattern #6

This pattern introduces "triplets." Triplets are groups of three. Clap three times for every beat in an even steady pattern. Triplets will be counted differently, count 1-2-3, 1-2-3, 1-2-3, 1-2-3 and clap along as shown below.

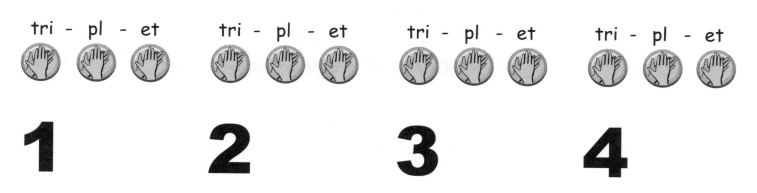

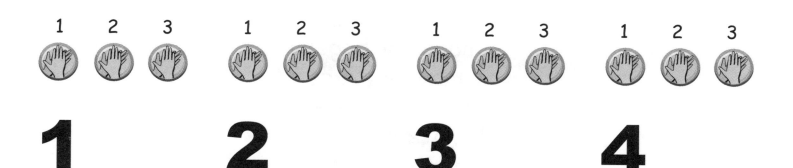

Parent / Teacher Notes

Counting 1-2-3 along with the clapping will help the children hear and understand the timing of triplets. Explain that triplets are groups of 3 notes within one beat. So if they tap their foot, every time the foot hits the ground will be on the one count.

Singing a Melody
Parts of My Body Song

These are the parts of my body from head, to my toes
I'm gonna move each body
part and say it here we go!
I move my head
I move my eyes
I move my nose
I move my ears
I move my mouth
I move my neck
I move my shoulders
I move my stomach
I move my arms
I move my elbows
I move my hands
I move my fingers
I move my legs
I move my knees
I move my feet
I move my toes

Parent / Teacher Notes

This is another fun song in a light rap style that will help children learn about the parts of their body while moving the body in time along with the music to get the body clock ticking. Make sure they move or point to each body part as it comes up in the song.

Nursery Rhymes
Mary, Mary Quite Contrary

Here is another fun rhyme to clap along to.

Mary, Mary, quite contrary,
How does your garden grow?
With silver bells, and cockle shells,
And pretty maids all in a row.

Parent / Teacher Notes

You can clap along with this rhyme on the counts of 1 – 2 – 3 – 4 with the children. It is a short rhythm so you can repeat it several times along with the children.

Fun Singing #4

For the next singing exercise, you will sing all the vowels. Make sure to shape your mouth to each vowel as shown below.

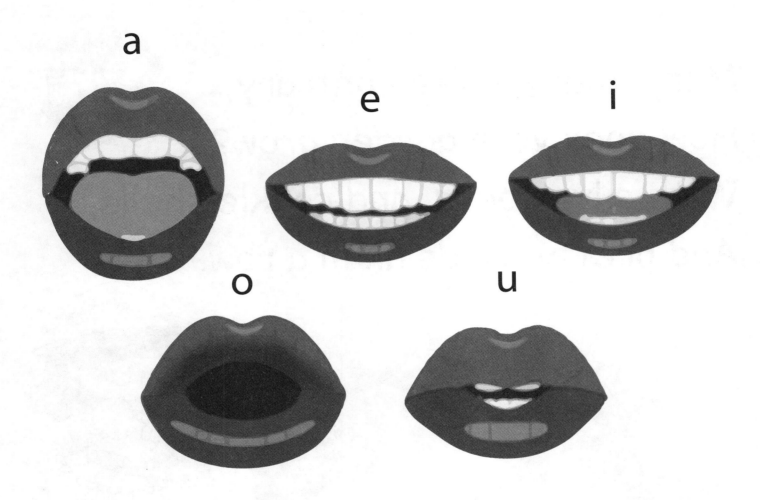

a

e

i

o

u

Parent / Teacher Notes

This is a very important lesson to help children excel in singing. The shaping of the mouth and lips singing vowels will help make words very distinct. Over accentuate the shape of the mouth for each vowel with the children.

Clap & Tap Pattern #7

The next clapping pattern will use a uneven shuffle rhythm. Listen to the audio track to hear the patterns rhythm and clap along.

Parent / Teacher Notes

Use the audio track to hear the rhythm for this lesson. The shuffle rhythm is used in blues music often. Have the children rock from side to side as they work on this pattern. This will help them to feel the rhythm. Notice that the clap is on the second of the two in each pattern. Have the children also tap their foot on the 1 – 2 – 3 – 4 while clapping.

Rock Star

In this section, there will be basic music lessons outlined that you can go through with children for piano, guitar, ukulele and drums. If you don't have these instruments at home, you can still go through the fun facts and worksheets for each. You can also start the children learning without instruments by using a few alternatives to see their interest. The following are a few ways to get started without instruments.

<u>Piano</u> – You can find free piano keyboard apps that can be used on iPad or phones that will allow the children to play notes in patterns. This will give them a start to piano fingerings and sounds.

<u>Ukulele and Guitar</u> – Guitar picks are used for both instruments and are very inexpensive. By just having the pick and learning the proper way to hold it can give the child a sense of how the instrument is played. Beginner ukuleles are very inexpensive and the basic foundation of guitar can be learned with the ukulele as well.

<u>Drums</u> – A drum set is a bit of an investment but you can make a pillow drum set at home very easily to see if your child has interest in this instrument. You would only need to purchase a pair of drum sticks to use. Arrange three or four pillows in a circle and have the children use these to play the patterns in the lessons.

Fun Facts, Learning About Instruments Piano

- The piano was invented in Italy in 1709 by a harpsichord maker.
- The word piano is the shortened version of the word pianoforte, which means soft (piano) and loud (forte).
- Pianos have a total of 88 black and white keys. Electric keyboards come in less key variations.
- Wow! The piano has the widest range of notes from high to low of all instruments.
- The piano can play accompaniment and melody at the same time.
- The piano has over 12,000 parts, 10,000 are moving.
- The piano can be considered both a string and percussion instrument. (Most categorize it as a percussion instrument because hammers strike the strings inside to produce sound.)
- Up until the 1950s, piano keys were made from elephant tusks. Today, in order to protect and preserve elephants, most piano keys are made from plastic.

Your First Lessons with Piano

Before you start your first lessons on piano you must learn the finger numbers for both hands. You fingers are numbered different for other instruments so make sure to pay close attention here. Use the following diagram and accompanying work sheet to have each child learn the finger numbers.

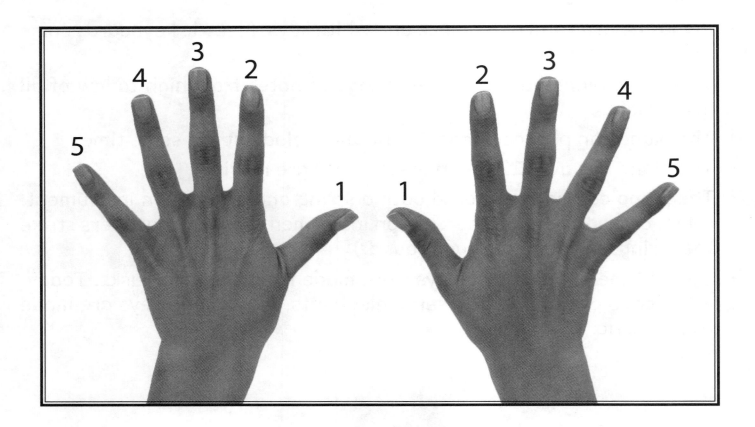

Lesson 1
The Keyboard Layout

The first thing you need to learn is the way the piano keyboard is formed so you can locate any note. Notice that there is a pattern with the black keys, going from left to right they are in groups of two and three keys. For this lesson simply just point to all the groups of two keys across the keyboard and then point to each group of three keys across the keyboard.

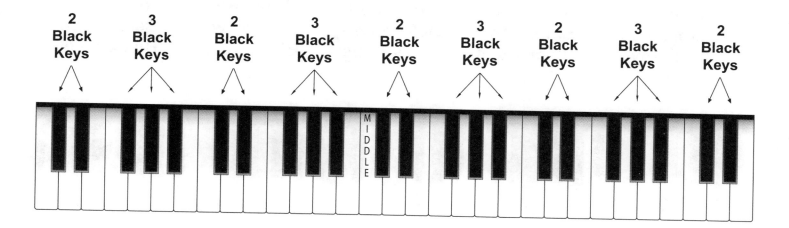

Lesson 2
Finding the C Notes and Middle C

Now you can find all the C notes across the keyboard, locate the white key before the first black key in every two black key group. Use the following diagram to correctly locate all the C notes on your keyboard.

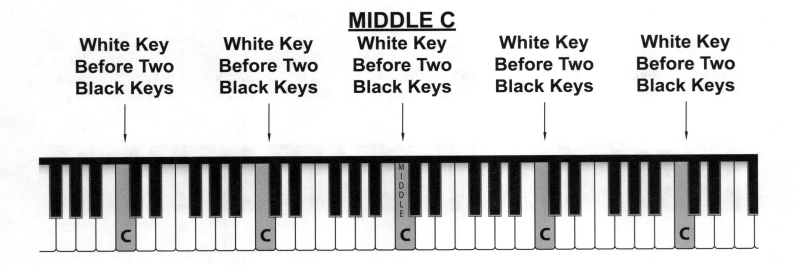

Lesson 3
C - D - E

Now you will play the C, D and E notes across the keyboard. Starting from every C note on the keyboard play the next two notes which are D and E. Play the C, D and E notes using your right hand thumb (C), index finger (D) and middle finger (E) in this order across the keyboard. Try not to have any two notes held down at the same time, each note should be played independently. Use the following diagram to help guide you to play the C, D and E notes.

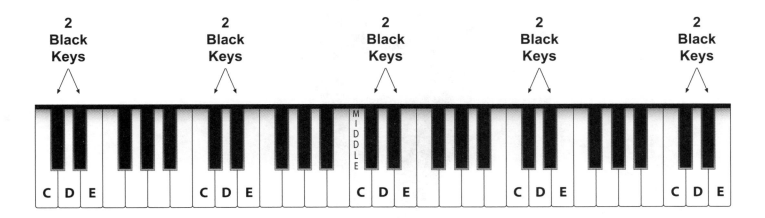

Lesson 4
Right Hand Notes Up From Middle C

Now you will expand two more notes to play the first five notes up from middle C. Starting with your thumb on middle C, play the next four white key notes in order using the next finger for each. Make sure to use the diagram to guide you to play the correct notes with the correct finger.

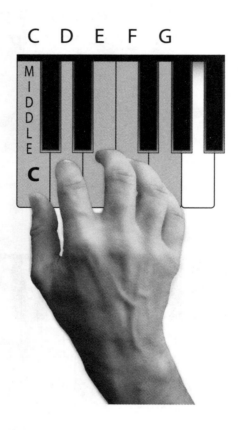

Lesson 5
Playing Two Notes Together

Next you will play two notes together which is an interval or mini chord. Start with your thumb on the middle C note then add your middle finger on the E note. Push these two notes down together in one swift motion and repeat this until you are comfortable with the motion and coordination.

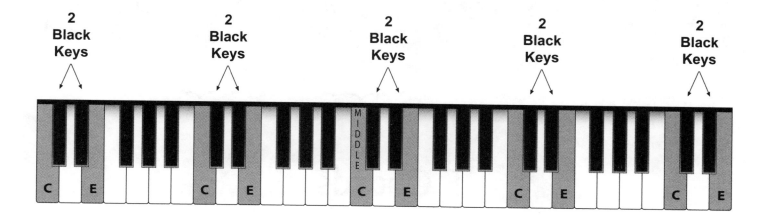

Lesson 6
The C and F Chords

Get excited you will now learn your first chords! For the C chord you play the middle C with your thumb, the E note with your middle finger and the G note with your pinky finger.

C Chords

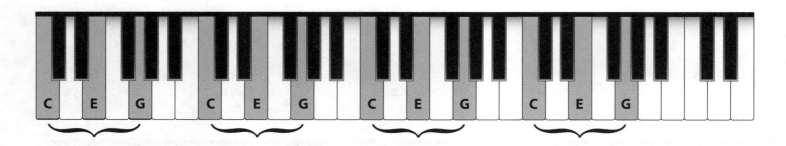

F Chords

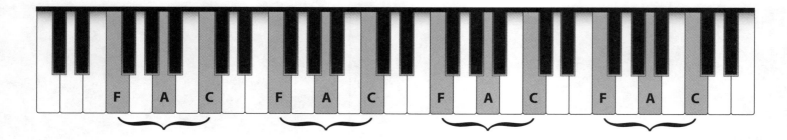

Fun Facts, Learning About Instruments
Guitar

- Most guitars have 6 strings from highest pitch to lowest are named
  E – B – G – D – A - E
- There are two basic types of guitars – Acoustic and Electric.
- The three main sections of a guitar are the body, neck and headstock.
- Guitars were always constructed with hollow bodies, until solid body
  electric guitars came in the 1950's.
- Gibson made his first electric guitar in 1936.

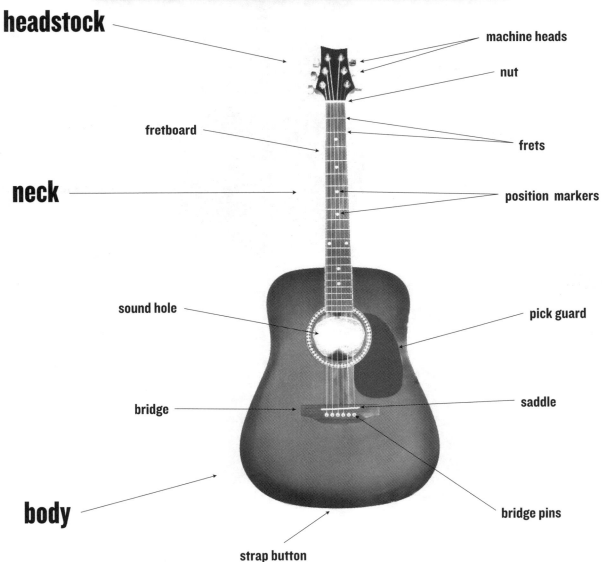

ELECTRIC GUITAR

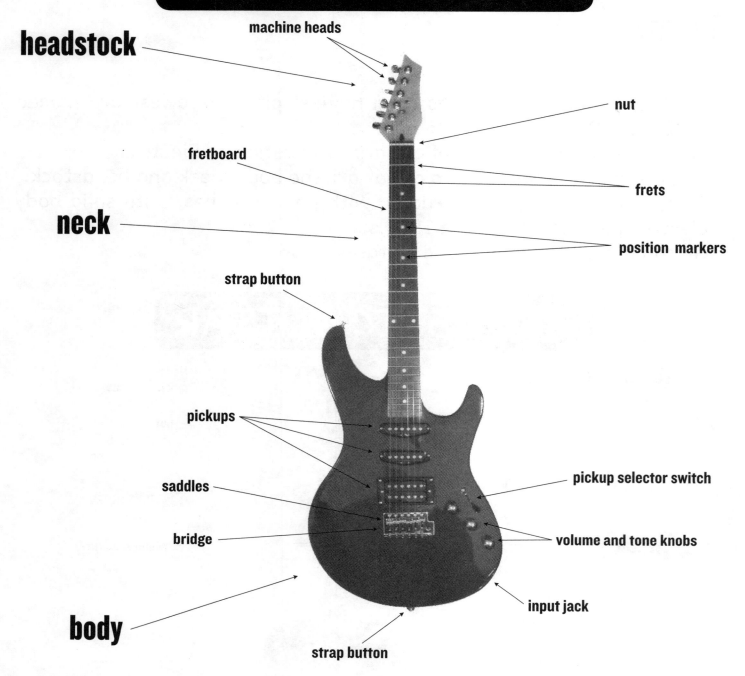

headstock

machine heads

nut

fretboard

frets

neck

position markers

strap button

pickups

pickup selector switch

saddles

bridge

volume and tone knobs

input jack

body

strap button

Your First Lessons with Guitar
Lesson 1
Holding the Guitar and Pick

Hold the guitar as shown in the picture. Make sure to have the neck slightly pointed upward. The fretting hand will be around the neck at the end near the headstock.

To play the guitar we will be using a pick. Hold the pick between your thumb and index finger, keep the other three fingers open and not in a fist as shown in the picture. It is very important to hold the guitar and pick properly to learn the basics of guitar quickly and easily.

Lesson 2
Picking Each String

Now that you know how to hold the guitar and pick properly lets do some playing! For this lesson you will pick each string. Start with the thinnest string closest to the floor and pick this string four times. Next do the same on the remaining five strings.

Alternate picking is picking down and up in a repetitive motion on a string. Pick each string using alternate picking until you feel comfortable with this motion.

Lesson 3
Strumming

Strumming is when you take the pick and in one motion brush it across all the strings. Strum all six strings down and count 1 – 2 – 3 – 4 and repeat this motion. Make sure the arm and wrist are loose and relaxed.

Next you will apply alternate strumming which is a down-up motion brushing the pick across the strings. Again keep your hand and wrist loose and relaxed.

Lesson 4
Fretting Notes

Now you will get your fretting hand into the mix. You will play your first chords. Here are the instructions for each chord.

G Chord – Put the 3rd finger on the 3rd fret of the 1st string. Arch your finger and use the tip to press down the note. Strum the skinniest three strings down.

GM7 Chord – Put the 2nd finger on the 2nd fret of the 1st string. Arch your finger and use the tip to press down the note. Strum the skinniest three strings down.

G7 Chord – Put the 1st finger on the 1st fret of the 1st string. Arch your finger and use the tip to press down the note. Strum the skinniest three strings down.

Now play a progression by strumming each chord four times.

Fun Facts, Learning About Instruments
Drums

Drums are fun percussion instrument found in almost every band from classical orchestras to rock bands.

- The hitting surface of a drum is called the "Drum Head."
- On a drum set the big low-pitched drum that sits on the floor and played with a foot pedal is called the Bass drum.
- The Snare drum has a rattle sound to it created by metal wires strapped against the bottom head.
- Drum sticks are used to play the drums.
- Drums were with us from the beginning of mankind.
- Drum sets were first used in the early 1900's.
- Brushes that create softer drum sound were used in drumming ever since 1920s.
- Drums are the most important part of the rhythm section of any band.
- Average drum sets have 5 pieces – Bass drum, Snare drum, two Toms, and Floor Tom. Several cymbals are also used (Crash, Hi-Hat and Ride).
- Drummers have to use both hands and feet to play different drums.
- Drummers need to have hand/feet independence, eye-hand coordination and good sense of rhythm.
- Drumming burns more calories in half hour session than cycling, weight lifting and hiking.
- Drumming is the oldest musical activity.

Your First Lessons with Drums
Lesson 1
Parts of the Drum Set

The two most important parts of the drum set are the Bass drum and Snare drum. The Bass drum is the biggest drum that sits on the floor. You use a pedal to sound this drum. The Bass drum is like the "Tapping" from the exercises in the book. The Snare drums sits face up in front of you and it has a rattle vibrating sound. This is the same as the "Clapping" from the exercises in the book. Look at the picture for the other drum parts.

Lesson 2
Holding the Drum Sticks

Having the proper grip on the drum sticks is important before you start playing. Hold each stick with the thumb pointing up the stick as shown in the picture. Don't grip the stick too tight keep a loose grip on the stick.

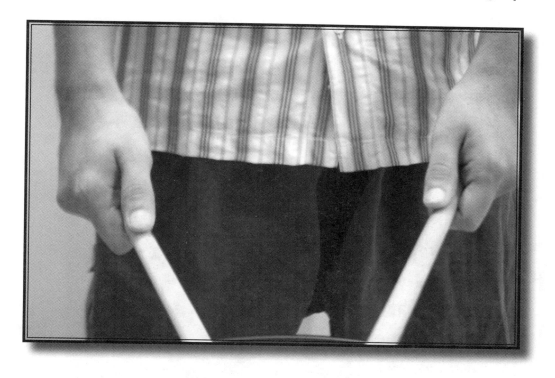

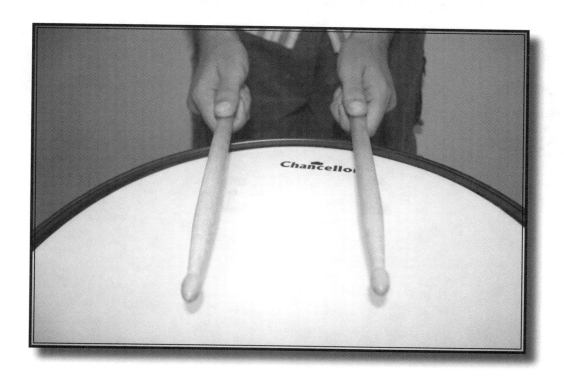

Lesson 3
4 On the Floor, Playing the Bass Drum

To play the Bass drum you need to use the bass foot pedal. Many children have a hard time with the concept of pushing the pedal down, they want to kick forward into the drum. Have the children play the Bass drum and count to 4 along.

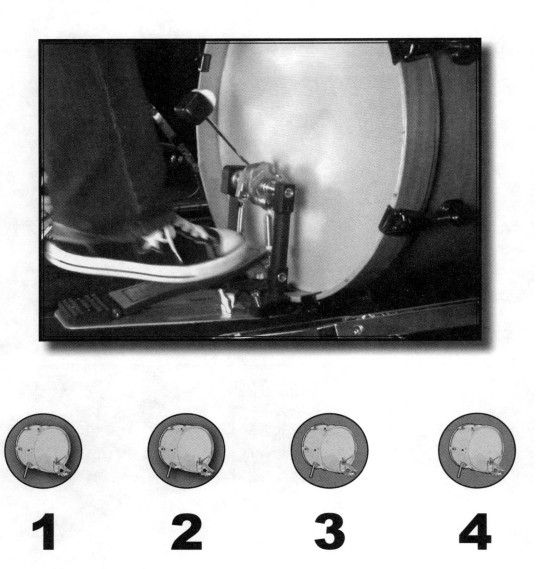

1   **2**   **3**   **4**

Lesson 4
The Snare, Hi-Hat Crossover

The next step is to play the Snare and Hi-Hat together. To do this cross the right hand over the left to play the Hi-Hat while the left hand plays the Snare drum. Play these two together repetitively while counting 1 – 2 – 3 – 4.

1   **2**   **3**   **4**

Lesson 5
Bass-Together

Bass – Together is the first drum beat. Play the Bass drum on beats 1 & 3 and the Snare/Hi-Hat on beats 2 & 4. Continue to say Bass-Together as the children play the beat. Once they can play this easily apply the beat to any songs that the children like.

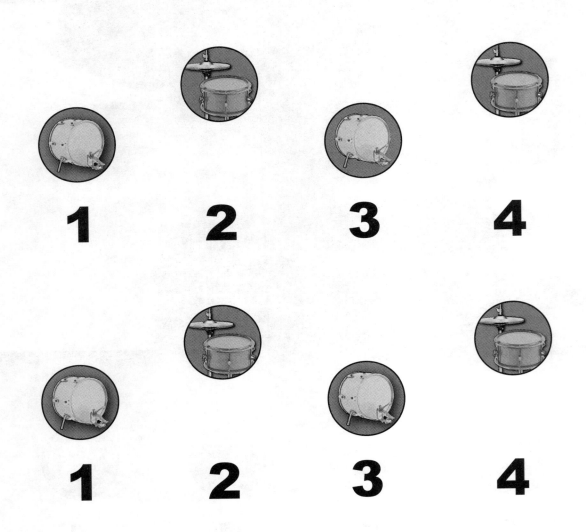

Lesson 6
Bass – Together, Bass – Bass – Together

This second beat is and extension of the last one. We are just adding a 2nd Bass drum after beat 3. Again play this beat along with a song once the child has it perfected.

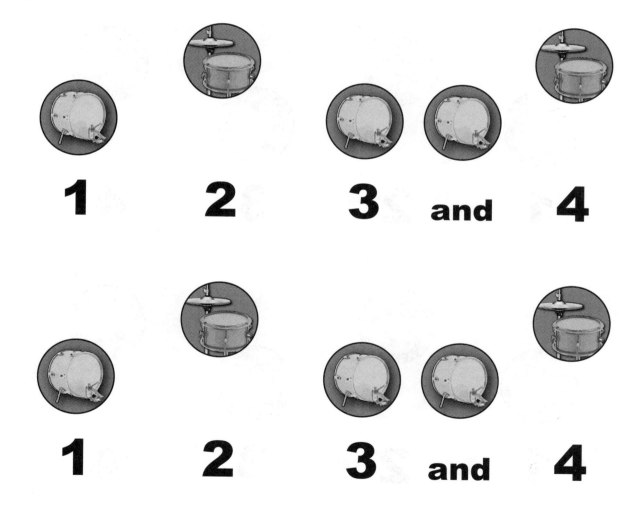

Lesson 7
Bass & Hi-Hat, Snare & Hi-Hat

This beat is a bit more complicated and requires more coordination. We are combining foot and hand patterns. The first hit will be the Bass and the Hi-Hat played together and the second hit will be the Snare and Hi-Hat played together. This is a common beat used in many songs!

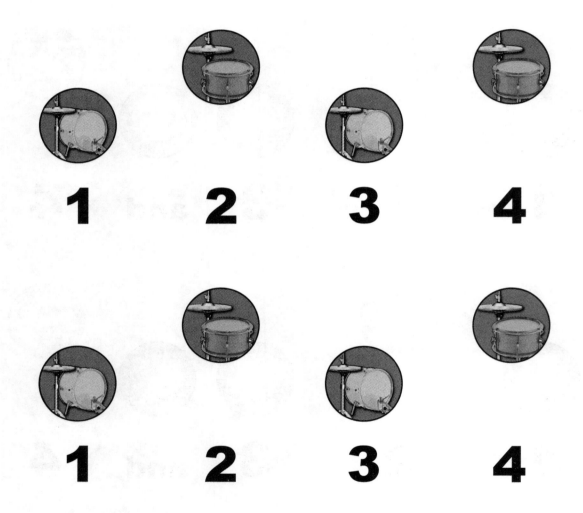

Fun Facts, Learning About Instruments Ukulele

- The name "Ukulele" means "jumping flea" in Hawaiian.
- The Ukulele is best known for its part in Hawaiian music.
- The Ukulele is commonly known as the "Uke".
- Ukuleles come in four different sizes - soprano, concert, tenor and baritone.
- The soprano is the standard size ukulele.
- Tiny Tim brought ukulele playing to the pop charts with his 1968 hit single "Tiptoe Through the Tulips."
- There are now electric ukuleles.
- The first ukulele was made in 1879.
- The 4 strings of a ukulele are tuned from top to bottom G-C-E-A.

Your First Lessons with Ukulele
Lesson 1
Holding the Ukulele and Pick

Hold the ukulele as shown in the picture. Make sure to have the neck slightly pointed upward. The fretting hand will be around the neck at the end near the headstock.

To play the ukulele we will be using a pick. Hold the pick between your thumb and index finger, keep the other three fingers open and not in a fist as shown in the picture. It is very important to hold the ukulele and pick properly to learn the basics of ukulele quickly and easily.

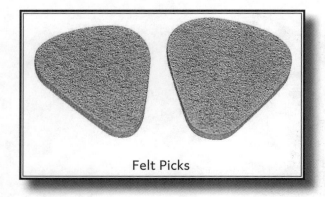

Felt Picks

Lesson 2
Picking Each String

Now that you know how to hold the guitar and pick properly lets do some playing! For this lesson you will pick each string. Start with the thinnest string closest to the floor and pick this string four times. Next do the same on the remaining strings.

Alternate picking is picking down and up in a repetitive motion on a string. Pick each string using alternate picking until you feel comfortable with this motion.

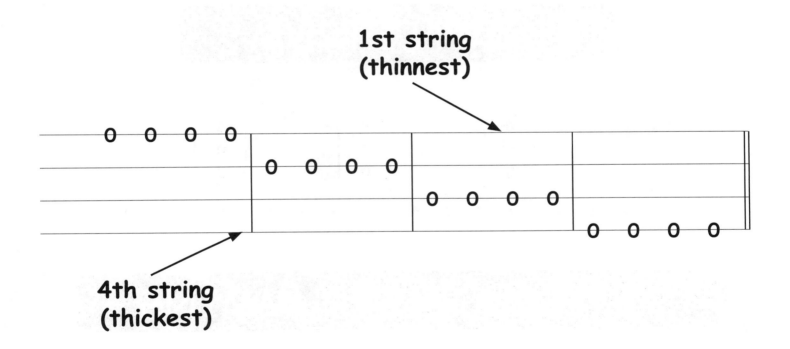

Lesson 3
Strumming

Strumming is when you take the pick and in one motion brush it across all of the strings. Strum all four stings down and count 1 – 2 – 3 – 4 and repeat this motion. Make sure the arm and wrist are loose and relaxed.

Next you will apply alternate strumming which is a down-up motion brushing the pick across the strings. Again keep your hand and wrist loose and relaxed.

DOWN STRUM

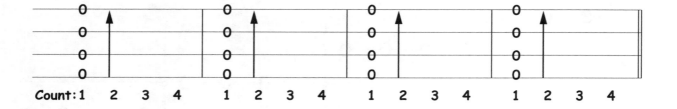

ALTERNATE STRUMMING

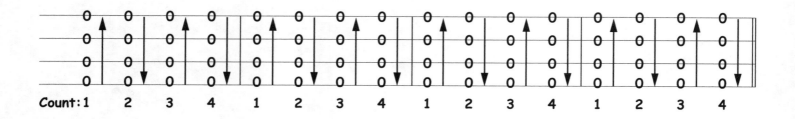

Lesson 4
Fretting Notes

Now you will get your fretting hand into the mix. You will play your first chords. Here are the instructions for each chord.

G Chord – Put the 3rd finger on the 3rd fret of the 1st string. Arch your finger and use the tip to press down the note. Strum the skinniest three strings down.

GM7 Chord - Put the 2nd finger on the 2nd fret of the 1st string. Arch your finger and use the tip to press down the note. Strum the skinniest three strings down.

G7 Chord - Put the 1st finger on the 1st fret of the 1st string. Arch your finger and use the tip to press down the note. Strum the skinniest three strings down.

Now play a progression by strumming each chord four times.

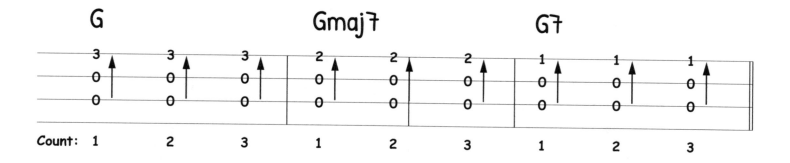

Making Instruments at Home

It's easy to make instruments using common, everyday objects you might have at home already. In this section, we'll give you just a few examples of how to make your own instruments.

Wood Blocks

You may already have a set of regular building blocks that contain two that you can use as instruments. You can also take an old broom and have an adult carefully saw it into pieces and sand down the edges to make your wood blocks.

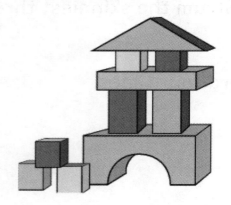

Shakers

A shaker can be made from a disposable coffee cup. You can put many different things inside the cup that will shake and create different sounds. Try using coins, coffee beans, jelly beans or pebbles.

DRUMS

Any sturdy box can be used as a drum. Different sizes and shapes will create different sounds. A round hat box makes a good drum. Round oatmeal or cereal boxes also make great drums. You can take two boxes and tape them together to create a set of drums.

Finger Numbers

Name: _____

Fill in the blanks in the diagrams below:

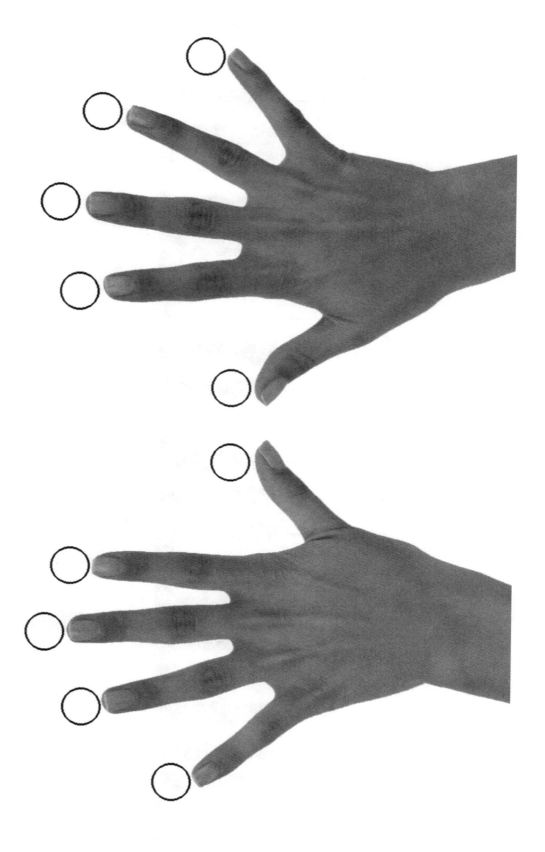

The Musical Alphabet

Name: _____

Fill the notes in on the keyboard diagram below:

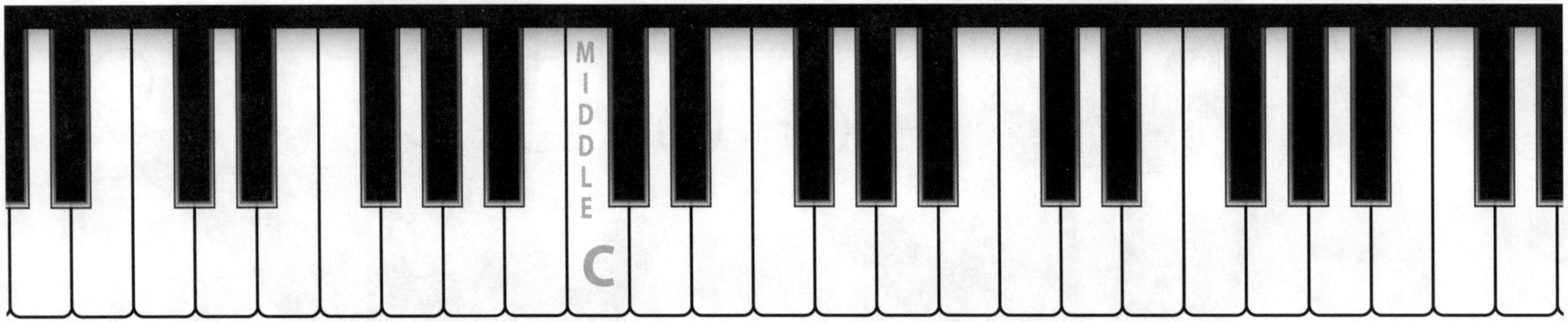

Right Hand Notes Up From Middle C

Name:_____

Fill in the note names below:

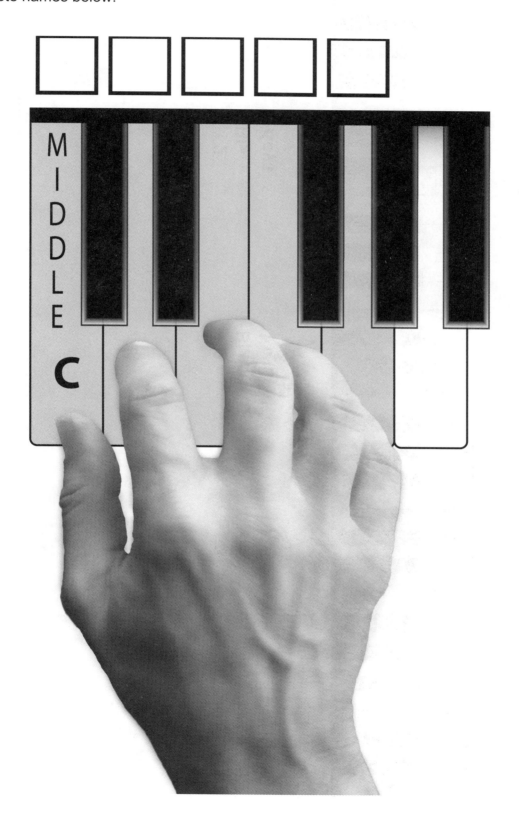

White Key Names Around Two Black Keys

Name: _____

Fill in the note names below:

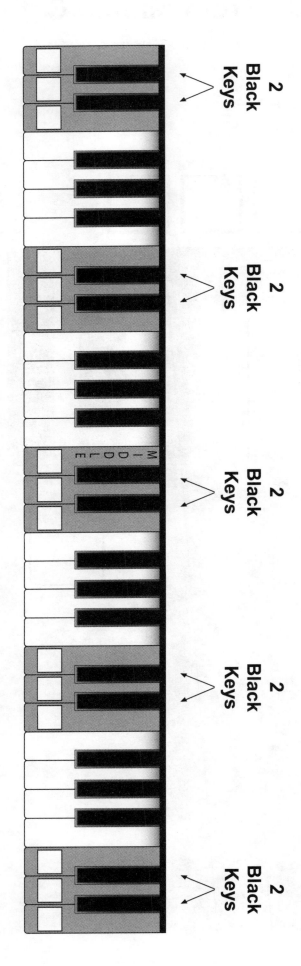

2
Black
Keys

2
Black
Keys

2
Black
Keys

2
Black
Keys

2
Black
Keys

White Key Names Around Three Black Keys

Name: _____

Fill in the note names below:

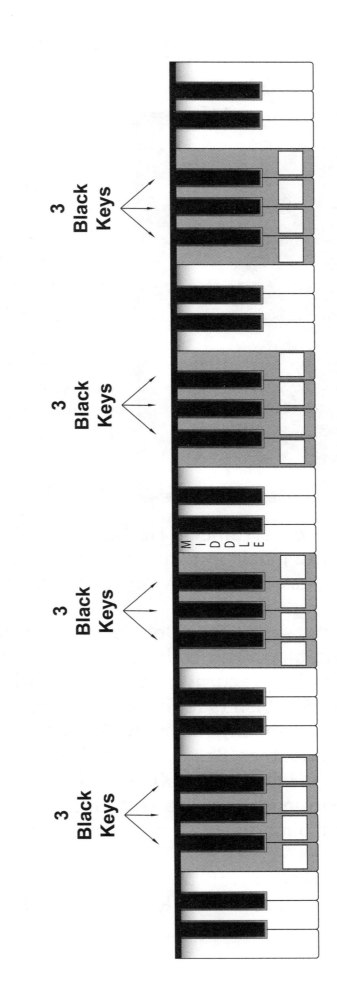

About The Author

John McCarthy
Creator of
The Rock House Method

John is the creator of The Rock House Method®, the world's leading musical instruction system. Over his 25 plus year career, he has written, produced and/or appeared in more than 100 instructional products. Millions of people around the world have learned to play music using John's easy-to-follow, accelerated programs.

John is a virtuoso musician who has worked with some of the industry's most legendary entertainers. He has the ability to break down, teach and communicate music in a manner that motivates and inspires others to achieve their dreams of playing an instrument.

As a musician and songwriter, John blends together a unique style of rock, metal, funk and blues in a collage of melodic compositions. Throughout his career, John has recorded and performed with renowned musicians including Doug Wimbish (Joe Satriani, Living Colour, The Rolling Stones, Madonna, Annie Lennox), Grammy Winner Leo Nocentelli, Rock & Roll Hall of Fame inductees Bernie Worrell and Jerome "Big Foot" Brailey, Freekbass, Gary Hoey, Bobby Kimball, David Ellefson (founding member of seven time Grammy nominee Megadeth), Will Calhoun (B.B. King, Mick Jagger and Paul Simon), Gus G of Ozzy and many more.

To get more information about John McCarthy, his music and his instructional products visit RockHouseSchool.com.